Foll

MW00873762

www.threepandasllc.com

www.thehusbandjournal.com

https://www.facebook.com/thehusbandjournal/

https://www.instagram.com/thehusbandjournal/

https://twitter.com/Husband_Journal

Special Thanks

I would like to say a special thank you to all of my friends and family. Many of you have watched me learn and grow through all of my mistakes. You have been my confidants and spiritual counselors during this process. Lisa, thank you for reminding me that all of this was "necessary". Monique, thank you for taking time to read this book and giving me your feedback. ShaCon, you have been a very important part of this journey. Through you, I have learned a lot about myself.

Thank you to my beautiful daughters who have helped me become a better person each day, Jalia and Jayla. Both of you are the light of my life. I could not be where I am without you. Thanks to my dad and brother for being my security blankets and sometimes enforcement.

A special thanks to spiritual family at Hope for Tomorrow Deliverance Center in Decatur, GA. Thank you for your counsel and guidance during a very dark time in my life. Pastors Calvin McCoy Jr., Co-Pastor Donnis McCoy, and church mother extraordinaire, Momma Flossie McCoy – Perry, I appreciate each of you beyond measure. Thank you to my spiritual mother Ms. Mary McCoy. You have held me down in prayer like no one else.

Preface

My brethren, count it all joy when you fall into various trials, knowing that the testing of your faith produces patience. *"But let patience have its perfect work, that you may be perfect and complete, lacking nothing" ~ James 1:2 – 4.*

We will go through trials; there is no doubt about it. Often we feel afraid, isolated, and embarrassed during those trials. The weight of that difficult time feels insurmountable. But if we allow God to do His perfect work within us, those trials to make us better, expose our weaknesses, and strengthen our relationship with God. So that in the end, we can claim the victory and count it as joy! We will be complete and lacking nothing at the end of it. We will know how to be patient and to endure trials, even in the midst. God allows things to happen in our lives that we do not understand, but through it all remember that He has promised you that He will always take good care of you.

I have gone through a lot of trials since my husband passed away in 2004. My most difficult trial has been my relationships with men. I seem to continuously make bad choices because I become frustrated with God in the process. I feel like His timing isn't fast enough. Then I completely shut off the idea of dating and close myself off from the possibility of meeting the right person.

It wasn't until the end of my last relationship that I began to write this book. I had to take a long, hard look at myself. I needed to be accountable for what God had already revealed to me. God showed me how to use my pain and experience to grow in Him. He has taken something that was meant to destroy me and turned it around for my good. Through the process of writing this book, I have learned that God always has my best interest in mind, He as protected me from so many things that I prayed for although they were against His will, and He has a perfect plan for my life. I pray that as you read this book, it helps with the pain that you are going through. By sharing my story I hope you will be able to hear God's voice speaking clearly into your life. With every turn of the page, reflect on where you are in your Spiritual journey in healing, align your will with God's will, and allow God to place the right man in your life. So count it all joy as you go through this journey. God loves you, and so do I.

Table of Contents

God Has Not Forgotten You

"Behold, the days are coming, says the Lord, when I will fulfill the good promise I have made to the house of Israel and the house of Judah" ~ Jeremiah 33:14 AMP. The first thing that I want to tell you is that **"God has not forgotten you!"** It definitely feels like it at times, but trust me when I say that He hasn't. It was during my first Daniel fast in January 2016 that I heard the voice of the Lord say to me that he has not forgotten me. Those words provided so much comfort and brought immediate tears to my eyes. The pressure of years of pain had come to a breaking point in my life.

I decided to begin the Daniel fast with my church for the first time. This fast consists primarily of eating fruits and vegetables just as Daniel did when he was under King Nebuchadnezzar *Daniel 1:12-15.* I have fasted other times, but never to this magnitude and for this long. Twenty-one days is a long time to go without meat or sweets. I added bread to my fasting as an extra measure of dedication. I was pressing the Lord for answers in my relationship with my boyfriend at that time. Things had gotten really off track with him. The longer I stayed in that relationship, the more I felt misguided. In short, I was in a toxic, verbally and mentally abusive relationship. I never imagined myself staying so long and permitting the abusive treatment that I had endured. He was a no-holds barred type of guy when it came to how he spoke to me. He would unleash such a barrage of insults and profanity that would break anyone's spirit instantaneously. I found out much later that he prided himself in being able to 'curse people out' and to make them feel worthless.

Just to give a little history about this relationship, he was someone I dated in high school. In all honesty, I knew he wasn't the right person for me back then. You can see a person's character early in life. I could tell that he did not have the same ambition, motivation, and drive that I had. He was barely making it through high school and was much rougher around the edges that I was. We dated briefly and ended up going our separate ways. A few years later he got locked up for a number of bad choices he'd made, in particular, he was hanging with the wrong crowd. I remember visiting him once when he was locked up. I left that place thinking, "God you saved me from something; you protected me!" God only knows what would have happened if I had been with him at the time that he got into trouble. My life would not be what it is today because of one bad decision.

Over the years, he always asked about me through one of our mutual friends. He shared with her how much he loved me and felt like we should have been married. Each time that I was pregnant by my husband, he told her that my daughters should have been his. After he was released, he made a life for himself. He got married, had a daughter, and tried to live as best he could with what he was given. He struggled to keep his marriage intact. He and I saw each other at our mutual friend's mother's birthday party about a year after my husband passed away. He was going through a divorce at the time. We tried dating again, but I had the same feeling about him that I remembered from high school. He still hadn't gotten very far in life and was barely making ends meet. Dating someone in high school is a lot different than dating them as an adult. As an adult, you see if the things you initially felt about them actually manifested. Let's be honest, we all are knuckle heads in high school. None of us had it completely together. Some of the people we thought would go on to be successfully end up being a complete dud in life, and vice versa. So I thought that maybe I had misjudged him in high school. Unfortunately, I had not!

My life had turned out completely opposite of his. I was mediocre, at best, in high school. I wasn't involved in any extracurricular activities, I didn't have stellar grades, and I had absolutely no plans beyond high school. I was enlisted in the Army as a last resort because I knew I couldn't stay at home any longer. My home life was extremely rocky, and I felt that staying in my parent's house beyond high school would only make things worse. While serving in the Army at Fort Gordon, GA, I met my husband. I felt from the very start that he was a perfect match for me. Reflecting on my relationship with him, I know it was ordained by God. My husband taught me so many things about life, finances, and love. I always tell people that he was wise beyond his years. I felt that he was the man I wanted to spend the rest of my life with, but unfortunately, that was not God's plan. In 2004, my husband passed away suddenly of cardiomyopathy. It is a rare, genetic heart disease that one out of four siblings inherits. He passed away at the age of 34. His death was one of the most devastating periods of my life.

Through it all, I managed to attain my bachelor's degree shortly before my husband's death. He and I shared two beautiful daughters, a lovely home, and lots of fun and exciting times together. We had so many plans for the future. After he passed away, I still managed to carry on and raise our daughters. I continued school to earn a master's degree, and I will soon be finishing my doctorate. I was able to provide stability in our daughter's lives. The girls and I continued to live in the same house, they were active in every sport and extracurricular activity possible, and now they are thriving young women. One has completed college, and she is working in her field. The other just began college and has completed her freshman year with all A's. I often tell them that their dad would be so proud of them. I know he is smiling down from heaven.

Throughout the years, I always felt like something was missing. I missed my husband tremendously. I would try to date here and there, but nothing serious. I did eventually get remarried, and it was a disaster. I realize now that I was looking for someone to fill my late husband's shoes, which is impossible. That is too much pressure for anyone. I picked a person that had serious emotional issues, and the pressure of his baggage along with mine was catastrophic. That marriage lasted less than a year.

So in 2014, my ex-boyfriend and I ran across each other on Facebook. We'd slightly kept up with one another, but didn't know what was going on in each other's lives. He would make witty or flirtatious comments on my posts occasionally, but it was nothing serious. Eventually, we started talking more on Facebook, then on the phone, and before long we were hanging out together. Finally, things progressed into a relationship. Initially, I felt that maybe God placed us in one another's lives again to give us another chance. Maybe what I felt about him the two previous times was wrong, or perhaps I had overlooked something in him. But as the saying goes, the third time's a charm....Right? When he shared with me how much he loved me and had always wanted us to be together, I just knew that this was of God. Maybe this was our time. I hoped that our story would be similar to the ones you see on television when the two people find each other, reconnect, and then they walk off into the sunset with their happily ever after moment.

Sitting on the other side of the situation and reflecting on all of the signs that God showed me, I feel foolish and ashamed. I know that he was not the right person for me. I knew it 25 years ago. During this third time of dating, I realized that my initial thoughts about him from high school were so accurate. He still wasn't motivated, he still had not accomplished anything in life, and he did not have any vision for his life. Let me keep it all the way real. He was living at home with his mother, he did not have a car, he had gotten into more legal and criminal trouble over the years, and therefore, he could not get a stable job. Whenever he got a halfway decent job, he would quit because he didn't want anyone telling him what to do. When our relationship began, he had a reason or "excuse" for all of the deficiencies in his life. Most of it was someone else's fault, but never really any of his fault. According to him, everyone in the world let him down to some degree or another. I believed the stories at first, and then I began to see through some of his lies and deceit. We started to argue constantly about him getting his life together, going to church, the numerous lies that I began to discover, and him constantly entertaining other women. The weight of this relationship was killing me. I had stopped doing all the things that were important to me like working out, writing my dissertation, and going to church. Most importantly, I had stopped putting God first. The thing about intuition (as some call it) or the Holy Spirit (as I **know** it to be) is that He will never lead us down the wrong path. He placed a still, small voice in my head in high school about this person. He had already protected me in this situation years ago. But in my mind, maybe God got it wrong. Maybe this is the person I'm supposed to be with, and I just had to prove it to God. Also, I felt like I deserved a boyfriend at this point in my life. I had patiently waited on the Lord, but it was taking Him too long. My previous marriage ended about two years before reconnecting with him, so it was about time for me to be happy as I saw my Facebook friends. I was tired of being lonely. **I felt like God had forgotten about me!** I was going to make my own destiny by dating someone that I knew loved me even though he wasn't exactly right for me. So I was trying desperately to make something work that I had no business entertaining in the first place.

On the second day of my fast, we broke up. I was wounded! I continued seeking God's healing and counsel during the fast. He and I had stopped speaking to one another, and I unfriended him on Facebook. I was overcome with grief from our relationship ending, and the brokenness of my other relationships and marriages compounded the situation. I was at my wits end. After about two weeks, I began to miss him more and more. On the morning of January 22, 2016, I got up, looked at an old picture of him, and was overcome with emotions. I ran into my bedroom closet where I could be alone with God and cry quietly so not to wake my daughters. I had begun praying in my closet after watching *"The War Room"* by Priscilla Shier. On that day in my tiny closet, my heartbroken soft cries became louder and louder. I sobbed so heavily that I'm surprised I didn't wake up my neighbors. Through the tears, I began a simple conversation with God. I couldn't stand the weight of living like this anymore. I couldn't bear losing another person that I cared about, or the embarrassment of another failed relationship. But this entire relationship was taking a toll on me. Not to mention, none of my previous relationships I had been in since my husband passed way lasted more than a year. It felt like I was cursed and God was punishing me for something. Maybe I was forgotten, or I didn't deserve to be in a happy relationship. I continued praying aloud, and the words began to pour out of my mouth faster and faster. As I spoke, the words changed from being clear and distinct, to muddled and running together. I was praying so hard and fast that the words began to sounds like another language. My words became more fluent and simply rolled off my tongue into long drawn out sentences. Suddenly it dawned on me that I was speaking in tongues. *"And they were all filled with the Holy Spirit and began to speak in other tongues, as the Spirit gave the utterance."* ~ *Acts 2:4 NKJV.* This was my first experience speaking in tongues or feeling so close to the Holy Spirit that I could actually sense His presence. It was as though I was conscious of my surroundings, but not in control of what was happening or what I was uttering. Through the streaming hot tears, I only paused to breathe and then resumed speaking fluently in tongues again. The more I spoke, the harder I cried. I wasn't in control of what I was saying, but as I continued speaking in the spirit, I could feel myself pouring out the issues on my heart and laying them down before God's feet. As I continued, I sensed that while I was releasing my burdens to God, He was picking them up one by one. Everything around me was at a standstill. I had no comprehension of time or of anything that was happening around me. All I knew is that in my prayer closet that morning, it was just me and the Holy Spirit. I had reached my breaking point. I bared it all to Him, and I was tired.

The reason why I had entered into that relationship and tried to create my own destiny is because, like so many of you reading this book, parts of my life are a mess. Since my husband's passing away, Satan has used my vulnerability and desperation for a husband to wound me again and again. After my husband died, I went from one broken relationship to another. I also peppered in a marriage that did not last more than a few months. I truly believe that, as I became more and more damaged, I left a trail of carnage behind me. As the saying goes "hurt people, hurt people." Some of the people I dated genuinely loved me, and others did not. For every person that came along and said the right words, I was willing to give it a shot. So by the time I entered the relationship with my ex-boyfriend, I felt that my past was so marred by my mistakes that there was no way anyone would ever love me, much less want to marry me. One guy from my past that I liked and actually wanted to date told me that I was damaged goods because I had already been remarried, so all we could ever be was friends. That small conversation left me devastated and heartbroken, so I felt like no one wanted me.

When I reconnected with my ex-boyfriend, he showered me with so much love and affection in the beginning that I felt he loved me beyond my mistakes. He knew all the right things to say and told me that he'd always wanted to marry me, which was exactly what I needed to hear coming off the heels of a barrage of major rejections and let downs. The fact that I was placed in the "friend category" by someone I liked previously and that all my transgressions were thrown in my face over and over again made me believe that I was undesirable. I felt like there wasn't anyone in this world that would want to take me seriously. Not only was this a gaping wound for the enemy to use against me, but it made me feel insecure and inadequate. I questioned God's intentions for my life all the time. Why was I the one who was always single? Why did my husband have to die? I had faith in every area of my life except when it came to relationships.

As a result, my attitude regarding men had become indifferent. Honestly, I could take them or leave them. I had become the shining example to all of my friends and family of a single mother making a successful living on her own. I had mastered the art of being a single parent and making it look good. On the outside, they thought that I was brave, strong, and unstoppable. But on the inside, I was broken, afraid, lonely, and angry. I used my strengths to camouflage my weaknesses as many of us do. I watched as several of my friends found love, went on dates, got married, and raised their kids via Facebook™. I pretended like it didn't bother me. I was genuinely happy for my friends, but I guess a sort of anger and jealousy was festering in my heart. How could God take my husband, and then wait so long to give me another one? He must have forgotten that I am here alone raising my daughters. The girls and I deserved someone to fill the void that was left by my late husband.

At every single school event, I felt cheated that my husband could not be there. Even worse, I couldn't even find a suitable man to help me. When things progressed with my ex-boyfriend and became serious, I thought that maybe this could be it. Maybe there was still a chance to be happy again. I poured my entire being into trying to make it work with him. I put up with the verbal abuse because no one else loved me like he did, or at least I told myself. I even convinced myself that some of the things he said were true, and maybe I was the problem in the relationship. When things began to deteriorate, I was thrust into a world of self-loathing again. God loved me, but He didn't love me enough to give me a husband.

At the end of my prayer, I felt God's calm, comforting presence around me. The Holy Spirit then began to speak through me in tongues. I could feel the atmosphere and dialog shift from all of my wounded pleas to His comforting answers and encouragement. His presence took over my spirit, and He was ministering to every ache and pain that I laid at His feet. As He spoke through me, the words were still in tongues. I could not understand them, but I could sense what the words meant. Then, the Holy Spirit's dialect changed from a foreign tongue to English as He continued speaking directly to me. The words were comprehendible, but they still were not my own. He told me so many things that comforted me in that moment. The three most important things that I would like to share in this book are, first He told me, "*I have not forgotten you.*" He repeated this sentence to me over and over again until it resonated in my heart and spirit. As I mentioned, I had felt forgotten and lost in the shuffle of life. My eyes still water when I think about this simple sentence and the impact it has on my life. It is an important statement for many reasons. We get caught up in our own desires, and we try to force our timeline on God. It's only after we make a complete mess of our lives that we cry out to Him for help. Sometimes, we try to play God in our own destiny because we think that God doesn't know what He's doing. Him simply reassuring me that He had not forgotten me was exactly what I needed to hear.

Secondly, He told me that the *"person He has for me will help me and not harm me."* He said that, *"He has a good husband for me."* This was poignant because I was hurting from so many things that happened in my previous relationships. I was lied to, talked down to, cheated on, and deceived. Under the stress and pain of this most recent relationship, I had lost myself. It was almost as if I was accepting the pain because I didn't think that God had something better for me. At that point, things had progressed into a full blown verbally and mentally abusive relationship. I had allowed someone that did not deserve five minutes of my time to get into my head and almost destroy me. But that day, God told me that the husband He has for me will not treat me like that. The man that God had chosen for me would be someone to build me up and not tear me down emotionally. The third thing He said was that, *"He is taking care of me and my girls."* God reassured me that we do not have to worry because we were under His protection. All three of these things helped to calm me down and comfort me.

In my conversation with the Holy Spirit, He also confirmed things to me that were in my heart about my ex-boyfriend. The most important thing God shared with me was that, *"he had the propensity to be violent, so that relationship was unsafe for me."* This message would be confirmed in prophesy spoken to me six months after this encounter and through other conversations that I had with our mutual friends. The Holy Spirit kept repeating that he wasn't good for me. He told me that the relationship was meant to destroy me. It would eventually kill me if I stayed. God showed me that He had been protecting me from my ex-boyfriend's violence. He revealed to me that Satan strategically set this up long ago when we were in high school. That's why I felt like he wasn't the right guy for so many years. On top of that, my dad and brother both had a similar feeling of dislike for him. They always felt that he wasn't on the same page as me and in some way sensed his propensity for violence. I recently asked my dad why he never liked him, and his response was simple. From the first day he met him, he felt many of the same things I did regarding his character, and he knew that he wasn't the right person for me. He also said he felt in his spirit like something wasn't right. He couldn't quite place his finger on exactly what it was, but he could sense that my ex was potentially violent and might kill or destroy me if I stayed in that relationship.

Despite all the warning signs and the voice of the Holy Spirit, I allowed Satan to enter my life. I got involved with someone that I knew wasn't right for me from the very beginning. I chose to create my own destiny instead of following God's path for my life which could have eventually cost me my life. But in the midst of it all, God still let me know that He was protecting me. I now see that entire relationship as a wake-up call. Without that experience, I might have still been on the wrong path, or I might have let that situation destroy or kill me. Even with God's warning, I did go back to him a few weeks later.

The Fruit on His Tree

As I got up one morning and went into my prayer closet, God brought a Bible verse to mind. *"You can identify them by their fruit, that is, by the way they act. Can you pick grapes from thornbushes or figs from thistle? A good tree produces good fruit, and a bad tree produces bad fruit. So every tree that does not produce good fruit is chopped down and thrown into the fire. Yes, just as you can identify a tree by its fruit, so you can identify people by their actions." Matthew 7: 16-20 NLT.*

At the end of my relationship, I was still very troubled by all of the events that took place. Like most people, I was trying my best to understand what happened and reevaluating my part in all of this. I also blamed myself for much of what went wrong. At times, I thought "maybe I should have let more things go instead of trying to confront them head-on," or I tried validating the relationship with things like "we did have some good times." Truly, when things were "good," they were really good. We enjoyed each other's company as long as things were going his way. If I questioned any of his actions or said anything that made him angry, the situation instantly went from "good" to "horrendous." He would begin a barrage of insults; especially when I would question him about keeping in contact with his ex-girlfriends. He would quickly let me know that I am not the boss of him and that my opinion of things was not relevant. He insulted my intelligence, my achievements in life, and me personally. He did everything in his power to verbally annihilate me. Each word that exited his lips felt like a punch to the face or stomach. I've heard over and over how verbal abuse is often worse than physical abuse because those words linger long after the relationship has ended. With each argument, I felt the tension in his voice escalate. The hair on the back of my neck would stand up as he screamed at me. Some of the verbal abuse was over the phone, and on a couple of occasions, it was in person. Things between he and I never escalated to the point of physical abuse because God was protecting me. There were a couple of times that I felt like we were very close to a physical altercation. I remember seeing the anger in his eyes and thinking "I could really get hurt in this situation." I later found out that he had been physically violent with one of his ex-girlfriends and his ex-wife. Thank God He protected me from his wrath becoming physical.

When he and I were not arguing, he was arguing with his ex-wife, his daughter, or even his mother. The things that I would hear him say to his mother were unbelievable. I remember going to his mother's house once, and she told me they had gotten into a very heated argument. I distinctly recall her telling me that he cursed her out like she was "a dog on the street." I was floored! I could never imagine talking to my parents or any person older than me in such a disgusting way. As the saying goes, if a man doesn't respect his mother he's not going to respect you.

As I finished my prayer and devotional, God told me to look at my old journals from a year ago. I kept these journals as reminders of things I've experienced and to help me grow spiritually, mentally and professionally. As I looked back, I noticed one distinct thing. I constantly questioned his character. My comments about him were more focused on his morals, values, and character than on anything else. Over the course of the year, I was not happy with the way I saw him treat other people. Even the general comments he would make while we were out in public sometimes made me cringe. The person that I thought I knew in high school and the person that was later revealed to me in this third attempt at a relationship were completely different. The side that he always revealed to me was sweet and loving in high school. He even spoke highly of his mother, and it seemed as though they had a close bond. He portrayed himself to be a caring and attentive son. Before our most recent attempt at dating, he never said a cross word to me, so I was perplexed when she told me about their argument. I realize now that I never really knew him. I only knew his "representative."

The most telling evidence of a person's character is how they treat their mother or father. My ex would literally curse his mother out on a regular basis. I sometimes witnessed his verbal abuse to her. At first, the things were gradual and seemed to be normal arguments. Usually, I would get off the phone with him once they got started. Then towards the end of our relationship, he would have full blown arguments with her or be completely disrespectful to her in front of me. I recall her telling me during one of our girl's outings at lunch that I could do much better than her son. I deserved someone that was on my level, and that would treat me much better than I had been treated by him. She even went on to say that she did not know how I had endured so much for so long. She loved me and wanted us to be together, but knew in her heart that I deserved so much more than what he had to offer. During one of our most recent conversations, his mother revealed to me that she was praying and reading her Bible one morning. She was asking God for help in dealing with her son because their arguments had gotten out of control. As she was about to pick up the phone to call him, it rang. It was him on the other end. She could tell that he had been crying. He began to tell her how much he loved her and how sorry he was for all the mean things he'd said to her over the years. As I listened, I thought to myself, "God is amazing! He's working it out." At this point, I don't know the progress in their relationship, but I do know that God is still in control. He will have the victory in this situation.

Jesus gave us an illustration in *Matthew 7* of the tree and its fruit. When you are getting to know a person, they can send their best "representative" to make you think they are a decent person. But what do their friends say about them? Do they put that person in high regard? Do they see that person as a good friend and overall person? How does that person's family look at them? Do they have the respect of their family members? Do your family members and friends approve of them? If you cannot find a single person, friend or family, that has good things to say, YOU HAD BETTER RUN! Remember that his friends and family know him best. They've seen all the games he's played, lies he's told, and people he's misrepresented himself to so if they are not his biggest fans, that's an obvious sign.

I laugh now at this epiphany, but in all seriousness, it can't be closer to the truth. It's such a simple concept, yet one that many women and men ignore. If a person's life is in shambles and stays that way, you know it's not their circumstances, it's the person. In my situation, my ex and I have many mutual friends. Some of those friends cautioned me about re-dating him. I distinctly remember my closest friend saying "Be careful!" In my mind, I thought "What in the world?" I was floored. She has known him longer than she's known me. She actually introduced us in high school. Although she loves us both, she warned me to be careful. I was the one that she cautioned. If that doesn't speak volumes, I don't know what does.

When you are entering a relationship, a person will only show you as much as you either want to see or as much as they will allow you to see. We have friends and family in our lives for a reason; they are here to protect us. They see things that are important in a person's character because we are wearing those proverbial rose-colored glasses. Many times, we take their advice and lay it aside just as I did with my dad and brother's advice. In all honesty, my dad doesn't like anyone, so his words were no surprise. But when the number of people warning you begin to add up, you'd better think long and hard about what you are doing. I don't think that all of our friends and loved ones are 100% right, it depends on the situation. But overall, they see things that we are too blind to acknowledge. The Holy Spirit not only gives us a warning, but He speaks to our loved ones as well. Maya Angelou said it best, "When someone shows you who they are; believe them." I would like to add that if the person's own mother warns about them, you'd better get out in a hurry…smh!

If He Doesn't Pray, He Can't Stay

One of the things I decided to do, when I began healing from all of the pain and rejection of my past, was to write. I've always loved journaling my thoughts. It is my therapy. I write down my thoughts to help me gather them and to keep me on track. I keep journals to use as a reflection of where I was a year or more ago. In particular, I write down my emotions, things I've overcome, and specific things that God has done for me. I don't ever want to forget how God has taken care of me and my daughters over the years. Since I do so much writing, one year my aunt encouraged me to make a list of all the things that I want in a husband. I had been single for a while and was ready to begin a new relationship. So while I was waiting, I began making a list of things that I wanted in my future husband. Of course, some of the things I included on the list were tall, dark, handsome, financially stable, well-groomed, own his house, have his own car, etc. Honestly, most of the things on the list were physical, materialist, and superficial. Besides, there is nothing wrong with being attracted to a particular type of person. When I reconnected with my ex, I abandoned most of the things on the list because he met "some" of the criteria like the physical traits. He was tall, dark, and handsome. I figured that we could work on the other goals like being financially stable, having his own car, and having his own place to stay. Besides, he reassured me that he was getting his own car in the next "few months" then he would move out of his mother's basement. Of course a "few months" never rolled around.

After he and I broke up, my aunt told me to go back to my list but to be very specific about what I truly wanted. The more I reflected on my past relationships, the more I thought about how the things I listed were good, but they did not speak of the true character of a person. The physical traits of the men that I dated in the past were important, but as you can see meaningless. They were all very handsome. Some were well established, or at least financially independent, and others were not. Some of them treated me very well, and others were out-right dogs. As I continued writing this list, I began to concentrate more on the personal characteristics of the man that I wanted to be my husband. It was more important to me that he is well respected by his friends and family, that he is a family-oriented man, and most importantly that he be a man of God.

So my list changed drastically. Now the first priority is that my husband has to be a Christian. I even posted a sticky note on my bathroom mirror that says "my husband loves the Lord; this is his best character trait" so that I would keep this in mind. His character has to exemplify his love and commitment to God. He has to be a man of true integrity. I know that doesn't mean that he's perfect. I am realistic in my expectations because I know that I am not perfect. However, it is realistic to want a man who has gone through his share of trials and continues to seek God's face in the midst of them. In his imperfections, he still seeks God! He allows God to counsel him in every area of his life, be it good or bad. Yes, looks and other physical traits are important because there has to be some type of physical attraction to spark a conversation. But the more I thought about it, the more I wanted my husband to be of good character. That is the man that's right for me!

So as I embraced my singlehood freedom again after trying again and again to make things work with my ex-boyfriend, I went out on a date. I was reluctant to go at first because he was a coworker. He would flirt with me occasionally at work as I played coy with him. At the time he was going through a divorce, and he was trying to get back into the dating scene. I must admit that he is a nice guy. He's very handsome, quiet, sweet, and very intelligent. When he told me that he liked me and asked me out, I thought I would give it a shot. We had a few mix-ups in our communication about where to meet and what we were going to do, but that was no biggie. We finally got our schedules together and decided to meet for dinner and a movie.

As the day approached for our date, I had about a million questions in my mind that I wanted to ask to keep the conversation going since I already knew that he was kind of quiet. If I was going to give this a shot, I wanted to take time to really get to know him outside of the office. Before I left, I said a brief prayer. I figured that it couldn't hurt to ask God to show me the things that I needed to see right away so that I didn't waste my time getting to know someone that wasn't right for me. Finally, we met up. He greeted me with a warm hug, and we walked into the restaurant to grab a table. He was a total gentleman. He held the door open for me, complimented me on my dress, and did all the right things. He began to tell me about his day and the fact that he'd gotten another job, but it was in a part of the state which is approximately two hours away. In my mind I thought, there's no way I'm starting a long distance relationship after all I've been through. That was my first red flag because I had dealt with the frustration of a long distance relationship in the past, so I knew that was definitely not what I wanted. I chuckled to myself "God definitely has a sense of humor when answering our prayers because the first thing out of this man's mouth was that he's moving two hours away."

We resumed the conversation and ordered our dinner. Once our food arrived, I stretched out my hands and asked him to pray over the food. The look on his face was astonishing. You would have thought that I asked him something completely vile or said something insulting or degrading to him. He reared back in his seat a bit and began to shake his head and stutter. At this point, I began thinking that he misunderstood me, so I asked again. When he was finally able to speak coherently, he insisted that I say the blessing because he didn't want to do it. I politely gazed at him, grabbed his hands, bowed my head, and closed my eyes to pray. As I was praying, I had a flash back on the times that I had gone out to eat with my ex-boyfriend. He would simply refuse to pray over our food. Later on in the relationship, my ex revealed that he is not a Christian. During one of his verbal tirades, he even revealed his disdain for all Christians and how he thought they were all fake and judgmental.

Although it is a small red flag, it's still one nonetheless. Remember when I revised my list, the top item is that my husband loves God and that he is a Christian. In my more specific list, I edited it to include a man that prays, that isn't ashamed to pray aloud, and that will lead me in prayer. I am very specific on the fact that my future husband must be unashamed in his prayer life. As I ended the prayer over our dinner, I looked up at my date. I heard a small still voice that said "he's not the one." In my mind, I thought to myself, "If he doesn't pray, he can't stay!" because it's on the list. We continued our conversation, but I quietly tucked away the millions of questions I had looming in my head to test our compatibility. For me, there was no point in asking because I knew that he wasn't the one for me. To this day, he does not know why I lost interest in him or why things never worked out. I chose to keep that my little secret. He did continue to call or text occasionally, and he would ask me out. Again, I politely declined his invitations.

I share this story not to make fun of anyone who may be shy or embarrassed to pray aloud. I have been there. I know many people who choose not to pray in public. Everyone is on an individual course in their relationship with God, so please do not take this as a personal judgement. But I know what I am seeking in a husband, and I have to see evidence of a prayer life. I went on another date with a different gentleman just a few days ago. As before, I prayed that God would reveal whether or not this man was right for me. Unlike the previous date, when the food arrived, he immediately reached out both of his hands to grab mine. Before I could even think about what was happening, he began to pray. The verdict is still out on him, but I was impressed with is inhibition to pray in public. That is definitely a good sign!

I am using this story to address a deeper issue with our choices in a potential mate. If we ask God for something specific, like a husband who is a Christian, loves Him, and puts Him first. Don't you think He's capable of doing it? And if the person that we are currently with isn't right, He will tell us that too. I feel like God heard my request and answered it immediately. He will never give me something that falls beneath what I ask. *Matthew 7: 9* continues to tell about God's answers to our requests, *"You parents – if your children ask for a loaf of bread, do you give them a stone instead? Or if they ask for a fish, do you give them a snake? Of course not! So if you sinful people know how to give good gifts to your children, how much more will your heavenly Father give good gifts to those who ask Him."* So we can expect God to give us the very best that He has to offer. More importantly, God won't give me someone that will lead me away from Him or that I have to coerce into prayer. I stand firmly on the fact that my future husband is a Christian man who loves God with all his heart. My faith is unwavering on that fact. So if someone is not exhibiting signs of a "God-fearing man," I need to take that as a sign that he is not my husband. I wavered on this in the past, and it got me nowhere. God will make the signs in our life clear, so please do not ignore them.

You Can't Carry Faith Holding That Baggage

When we think about faith, there are several Bible verses that come to mind. In particular, we default to *Hebrews 11:1* *"Now faith is the substance of things hoped for, the evidence of things not seen."* – *KJV*. We know that our faith is what determines what we have in life. And if we do not have enough faith, God gives us his grace to restore our faith. Every great sermon we hear on Sundays or read in inspirational books is founded on developing our faith in all areas of life and overcoming the fear that paralyzes us. We suffer from lack of faith and confidence throughout our lives. The Bible speaks of faith on numerous occasions, and even gives us timeless examples of how *"if ye have faith as a grain of a mustard seed, ye shall say unto this mountain, Remove hence to yonder place; and it shall remove; and nothing shall be impossible unto you."* – *Matthew 17:20 KJV*. So why is it that when we read the Word of God, listen to these sermons, and read our inspirational and motivational books we still return to our old habits of self-doubt and defeat?

As children, we come into this world not knowing or understanding that we cannot accomplish something. That is how so many broken bones, missing teeth, and exciting adventures occur. When we look at children or listen to their stories, we see their naivety and reminisce on that time in our lives. We didn't know that we could not do something until someone actually told us that we couldn't. We didn't know that we were not supposed to ask for whatever we wanted. We thought the world was ours to explore, and we threw caution to the wind. We spread our wings and flew as far as the wind would take us.

As some point in our minds, that halted. I don't think we realize exactly when we lost our naivety. For most of us, it was gradual. We had to grow up, take off the rose-colored glasses, and face reality. Life dealt us lessons in heartache, let downs, and so much more. This was the beginning of the systematic deterioration of our faith. So here we are reading books and quoting scripture to try to reprogram our brains to their original state.

My relationships were a testament to my lack of faith in God. I could have faith for my finances to improve, for a job promotion, and for any material possession I wanted. I trusted God to deliver me out of so many situations. If you needed a pep talk about having faith, I would always be the person to speak to and to help you get out of a funk. But in the most important area of my life, I doubted God and limited His authority because this is the most vulnerable area of my life. I was in control of my relationships and marriages until I was in trouble and needed God to bail me out. Time after time, I chose men that I thought would be a good fit for my life. Sometimes I purposefully choose men that were not in a place to fully commit to a relationship, so I didn't have to commit to them either, thus the long distance relationships and casual sex partners. Each person was just another casual encounter or hook up when needed. None of these situations lasted long because one of us grew tired or was ready to move to the next level. Whenever it was my turn to commit, I grew terrified at the thought. One of the unresolved issues in my life is the passing away of my first husband. Because of his untimely death, it created a lot of fear in me. Even to the point of not fully committing to someone because the thought of someone else other than my late husband or immediate family having authority over my remains frightened me. That fear only perpetuated my other relationship fears.

So here I sit dwelling on all of the past relationships that have chipped away at me. Each one left a huge dent in my heart and a bruise to my ego. Even the ones where I did the breaking up left some sort of damage. I was lugging around an enormous amount of old baggage. I carried it with me into each relationship. When I cried out to God that early morning in January 2016 and began to speak in tongues, I unloaded all of that baggage. Though my words were unintelligible, I could tell that every single bit of the ugly truth that I was hiding in my heart was coming out of my mouth. There was no more hiding. God heard all of it. So you would think that after that encounter, I would have enough faith to wait on God's ordained husband for me. Or maybe I would at least have enough sense to know that my encounter with God was real and that He was in control of my situation. The answer to that is no.

It was a few weeks after the Holy Spirit spoke to me in my prayer closet that I began to share with a few family members and friends about my encounter. They were amazed at such an awesome story. I reassured everyone that I would never go back to that situation since I'd heard from God himself. Well shortly after that, my ex-boyfriend sent me a text wishing me Happy Valentine's Day. We exchanged pleasantries, and I tried to keep the conversation light. A few days later, he called and before long we were speaking on a daily basis again. He was back into my life before I knew it. We decided to give it another try. I thought that maybe if I prayed for him to change his life and if I interceded on his behalf God would hear my pleas. God was capable of anything, right? So my faith was in the fact that God could change this situation from one that was meant to destroy me to one of hope. It would be the greatest love story ever. We began praying together every morning.

Well in actuality, I was praying and he was listening. Then immediately after the prayer, as he was driving, he would proceed to curse out every person in his way in traffic. As time went on, the morning prayers ended, and we went back to fighting. His verbal abuse became worse. With each time we tried to reconcile, he became more and more comfortable and free with his insults. I was even more heartbroken and devastated. God, why wasn't this working? We went through a cycle of being on and off again for four months until I had another encounter with God.

This time He used a student in one of my classes. Little did I know, but God was setting up something life changing. I was teaching an evening class at a local Christian university to supplement my income from daily teaching job. Typically I teach accounting and management courses, but this was an economics class. Because I'm not strong in that subject, I hated teaching it. Not only was I dreading the class, but I was constantly fighting with my ex-boyfriend. Earlier that afternoon before I got to work, I cried out to God once again.

This time my prayer was simple. I had been going back and forth with my ex for quite some time, and I was completely tired. I asked God to show me what to do because I was battling between my heart and my head. I had even found a meme earlier that day that depicted a man walking on a tight rope balancing a brain and a heart. Boy, if that wasn't me! I felt like I was in constant turmoil about which one to choose, my heart or my head. I know what God told me in January, but I know how my heart felt too. More specifically, I asked God to tell me exactly what to do because He knows my heart. I was so lost and confused. God made me with a caring heart that will not give up on people when I love them. I pleaded with God to give me some direction on what to do.

By the time I got to my evening class, I was emotionally drained. I did not feel like putting on a brave face, or playing the role of the Christian professor. Two of the ladies in my class were prior students, but there one student in particular that I had never met. He seemed very professional, studious, and quite. He's a pastor at a small church in Decatur,

Georgia. It is pretty common at this Christian university to instruct students who are pastors or who are affiliated with ministry in some manner. The first couple of weeks he shared some of his messages from his Sunday sermon during our devotional. One that inspired all of us in the class was regarding dealing with trials. He explained how we experience three stages of growth in life when we are going through trials. How we handle those stages determines whether we continue cycling through the stages or graduate. In the first stage, we must *"glory in tribulations also; knowing that tribulations worketh patience; And patience experience; and experience, hope. And hope maketh not ashamed; because the love of God is shed abroad on our hearts by the Holy Ghost which is given unto us." Romans 5: 3 – 5 KJV.* This means that we are going to experience tribulations in our lives, and we should expect them. Those tribulations are going to test our patience and hope. They are going to be in areas in our lives where we are most vulnerable. But God gives us what we need to overcome these tribulations. In the second stage we should *"think it not strange concerning the fiery trial which is to try you, as though some strange thing happened unto you:" I Peter 4:12.* So we should not be surprised by the test and trials. However, until we use what God has given us to pass the test in the second stage, we will continue to repeat it. It was around this moment that I sat down and began writing down the scriptures that he was quoting. His words spoke directly to my heart because I was being tested in my relationships. I could see where I was experiencing the same trials over and over again because I had not learned the necessary lessons from the previous relationship.

As he continued speaking, he gave us another scripture *"The heart is deceitful above all things, and desperately wicked: who can know it?" Jeremiah 17:9 KJV.* He began to tell us that we cannot trust our hearts to help us make decisions when we are going through tribulation because that will lead to us continuing to cycle in stage two. This was exactly where my battle was, between my heart and my head. We have to trust what God has told us in our heads (faith) and not rely on our hearts (emotions/fear). Once we pass the test in stage two, we move to the final stage where we experience God's perfect work in our lives. In stage three, *James 1: 2 – 4* says, "*My brethren, count it all joy when ye fall into divers temptations; knowing this, that the trying of your faith worketh patience. But let patience have her perfect work, that ye may be perfect and entire, wanting nothing.*" KJV or "*that you may be perfect and complete, lacking nothing*" NKJV. I was speechless! In my mind, I kept thinking that "I'm stuck in stage two!" Every relationship since my husband passed away had been a test of my stage two. I hadn't released my situation to God, so I kept repeating this stage. My faith was in myself and not in Him. That evening, I had gotten my answer from God. He heard my prayer again and answered it. His words gave me the courage to finally end my relationship for good.

The next week, as I got ready for class I was a bit more confident in my decision, but still had some reservations in my mind about completely ending things. That afternoon, as God was setting things up, Satan was working against Him. For some reason, I was extremely reluctant to go to class. Everything in my mind and body wanted to cancel that evening's session. I was irritated and felt ill-prepared to teach. One of the other students in the class even called me and said that she might be late for class. This fueled my interest in cancelling for the night. I distinctly remember telling her not to worry about coming to class if it was too much of a hassle because we were probably going to leave early, so she could just come next week to make up the work. When the time approached for class to begin, I grew more and more aggravated. As the students began to arrive, I devised a plan to discuss our devotional, lecture briefly, and dismiss the class early.

My spirit lightened as we began sharing how much we enjoyed my student's words of faith, hope, and inspiration from the previous week. We had all gained answers regarding our personal situations and thanked him for his message. I told him how his words personally helped to free me from my relationship. I shared with the class about my prayer from the previous week, and how the explanation of those three stages was the answer I needed to stop holding onto a relationship that was meant to destroy me. It was at this time that another lady in the class spoke about her situation, which was similar to mine. She shared how she had been conflicted with letting go of a long distance relationship, and needed an answer from God as well. My student thanked us graciously. While we continued talking about our experiences, the atmosphere began to shift. He began prophesying to us one by one. The Bible says, "*In the last days, God says, I will pour out my Spirit on all people. Your sons and daughters will prophesy, your young men will see visions, your old men will dream dreams. Even on my servants, both men and women, I will pour out my Spirit in those days, and they will prophesy "Acts 2: 17 – 18 NIV*. He was giving us direct messages about our lives from God. One other time in my life have I received a prophesy about my husband, and it was from my beautiful neighbor, Ms. Mary McCoy. She told me years ago that my husband was a very important man. He was either a doctor or a lawyer, and he was very educated. So in reality, I knew over the years that I was settling for less than what God had planned for me.

My student went on for two hours prophesying to each of us. He would move from one person to the next describing people or events in our lives. So even if we had some similarities in our situations, his details were specific enough for us to know that the message was for that individual. When he spoke to me, he first mentioned that he saw a brick wall with a stop sign. He could see a man tearing down the stop sign and stomping on it. After he finished kicking and stomping the stop sign, he began to tear down bricks in the wall. I can honestly say that my mouth was wide open at this point. I did have a wall around my heart before entering that relationship because I had been hurt and let down so many times. But I let my ex-boyfriend in because he told me how much he loved me and made me believe that I was not damaged goods. My ex reassured me that he would never treat me like the men of my past. My student could see the man taking pride in destroying my heart, almost as though it was a personal accomplishment. When I reflected on that statement, I thought about how I would beg my ex to stop speaking to me in such a cruel way, but he would keep going in such a way to show me that he could destroy me at any moment with his words. I recall times when he even bragged about how he had the power to destroy previous girlfriends with his words.

As I sat there soaking in his words, my student began speaking to one of the other ladies in the class again about her situation. His words for her were about a relationship in which she was conflicted. She carried around a lot of guilt, and was trying to decide whether this was God's will for her life. While some of the words he spoke to her were applicable to my situation as well, his prophesy was specific to her life. She too knew that the relationship was not right for her and that God has something much better once she lets go. This prophetic student then made it around to me again, this time he was even more direct. I will never forget these words. **"He is not your husband!"** Those were the words that made everything connect. I thought about God's prophesy to me in January

2016 in my prayer closet and all the things that were not right in that relationship. By this time I was shaking because I knew it was God reaffirming what I already knew.

Throughout our relationship, my ex kept telling me that he felt like we should be married. Whenever we went places in public, people would always assume that we were married. I recall going to a restaurant one afternoon with him, and our waiter asked if we were married. We answer "no" and asked him why he wanted to know. He proceeded to tell us that he reads people's energy and that our energy showed him that we should be married. So when my student said specifically that "He is not your husband," my mind flashed back to that day at the restaurant. Then my student proceeded to explain that I needed to completely separate from my ex. He said that he has a propensity for violence and that God had been protecting me. He stated that if I stayed, things were not going to end well for me, and he shared some very specific details about my ex that only I knew. He told me that God was going to deal with my ex and that he would be isolated while God was dealing with him. At this point, I was trembling and barely able to contain it. He told me that I need to separate from him immediately and that God had used this class as a set-up to get my attention. That's why I didn't want to come to class that night. God had it all planned out and the things that He shared with me in my pray closet on January 22, 2016 were aligned with what I heard on June 22, 2016. Yes, that's correct. It was six months to the day when God first spoke to me.

So there I sat in class knowing that everything that God told me was true. There was no more doubt in my mind about what to do. I had asked God for an answer, and there it was in my face. *James 1:5* says *"If any of you lacks wisdom, let him ask of God, who gives to all liberally and without reproach, and it will be given to him"* NKJV. He is not my husband! If I chose to disobey at this point, I was headed to an early grave. I was faced with so much damage and hurt by that situation, that I had no other choice but to give it all to God. I had to have faith that He would send me the man who is specifically ordained by Him to be my husband because after everything I had tried up to that point failed miserably. I had let fear stop me from believing God. I knew that my ex wasn't the right man for me long before my student prophesied it. I knew what could possibly happen to me if I stayed, but the fear of not finding a man or being alone for the rest of my life was drowning me.

He Is Not Your Husband

I want to take a minute to talk about this sentence for a moment, "He is not your husband!" Let that sentence soak into your spirit for a minute or two. When we reflect on our previous relationships, we tend to think about how much time we lost entertaining someone that wasn't right for us. I admit that I knew all along that my ex wasn't the right person for me, and I acknowledge that I continued down the wrong path until God had to literally come down from heaven Himself and stop me from entertaining the thought that he was my husband. He told me in my prayer closet in January. He sent numerous signs. Then six months later, He told me through my student. It wasn't until the exact words, "He is not your husband," came from his lips that I understood that I was in the wrong relationship.

Part of the reason I thought that he was my future husband was because he told me that for years and years he wanted us to eventually get married. He had always dreamt of us being married. He told me that although he had loved before, he had never been in love with another woman like he had with me. At the beginning of our relationship, I remember his mother sitting down and talking to us about how it was fate that we were given another chance. She cried tears of joy that we were able to reconnect. She expressed to me that she always liked me and thought that I was perfect for her son. Throughout our relationship whenever we'd breakup or have disagreements, she would tell me that she was praying that we would get back together and work things out. She began calling me her daughter-in-law, and claiming my daughters as her very own. I recall people assuming that we were husband and wife almost everywhere we went because of how we interacted with one another. It was like we complemented each other. As I mentioned in the previous chapter, just a few short months before we permanently broke up even our waiter at the restaurant asked if we were married because he said that our "energy" seemed like we were spiritually connected. All of these things lead me to believe that although I was going through pure hell with this man, we were still meant to be husband and wife despite my initial intuition and my encounter with the Holy Spirit.

Coming from a very human, raw, and realistic standpoint, I loved this man despite his shortcomings and all the signs. I loved him! The old saying goes; the heart wants what it wants. Whenever we were apart, I missed him. I would lie in bed for days crying my eyes out. I would fall into a deep depression which consisted of taking pain pills, muscle relaxers, or drinking to numb the pain. The hardest pill for me to swallow has been the solidified fact that no matter what I do, we are not meant to be together. Knowing that someone is not your husband does not always make it easy to walk away, honestly I think in some cases it makes it harder. It gives you the closure that you need, but it does not wash away the memories and love you once shared. We are still human, and we error in our ways. We love unconditionally, we avoid all the stop signs, we throw caution to the wind, we give until we have nothing left, and we leap in with hearts wide open for the person we truly love. God does give us some solace in the fact that we will love the wrong person, and honestly, that's okay because God still loves us and all of our mistakes. So as you reflect on the past relationships, remember that you are not together for a reason and that God loves you.

God later revealed why he wanted me out of that relationship. I found out the full story of the lies, cheating, and manipulation. My ex-boyfriend was still seeing an ex-girlfriend. He started seeing her while he and I were together, but I did not know it at the time. Shortly after I ended things with him, he moved in with her. This was the woman that he adamantly denied he was involved with and swore that he hated. Our last huge argument was over his dealings with her and continuing to follow her on social media. When I heard the news, it put a huge knot in my stomach and a knife in my heart. It always hurts to know that you gave effort to someone who so easily threw it away, but I feel this information was my last bit of closure. Shortly after they rekindled their relationship, it burned out. They got into an extremely volatile argument at work and broke up. Look at God!

This is what God was protecting me from, this is what God was trying to warn me about, and this is what God meant in His prophesy from my student. When God sends those thoughts or intuitions your way, it's because He knows all things. He is trying to warn you of the danger that is ahead. When you know that someone is not a right fit for your life or if God has told you numerous times through various signs that someone is not your husband, you can try to make it work as much as you'd like, but eventually, it will blow up in your face. Sometimes it will be a small incident, and sometimes it could cost your life. I don't know what signs you have experienced over the years. Maybe it has been a direct message from God, or maybe a small coincidence. It might be a slightly uneasy feeling, or it could be that their actions don't match their words. Either way, God forewarns us about each person we meet. Often those indicators begin as a small voice and gradually get louder and louder until we have no choice but to listen. I look back and think about the pain that could have been avoided if I had just listened to God back in January. I also think about how this could have been much worse if I had disobeyed God's warning and prophesy in June. The most important lesson in this situation is that there will always be a tug-of-war between the head and the heart, but in the scripture, it says that *"The heart is deceitful above all things, And desperately wicked; who can know it?" Jeremiah 17:9 so "Keep your heart with all diligence (or guard it), for out of it spring the issues of life" NKJV.* Letting go of someone that is not right for us requires a huge amount of faith and trust in God. We have to know that God's plan for us is far greater than the plan that we have for ourselves. Trust the signs that He gives you. They are there for a reason.

When I was choosing to follow my heart, I compromised my dignity and integrity to try to make something that was not ordained by God work. My daughters would hear me arguing with him over the phone. They even saw me cry over things that he said to me. The lowest point of that relationship was when I was supposed to go meet him after we had broken up the final time to get some of my things. He and I were discussing where we should meet over the phone. He was completely rude and nasty to me. I could hear nothing but hatred in his voice. As I talked to him, my entire body was shaking. I did not want to see his face or even be in his presence. We agreed to meet, and I headed toward the door to leave. As I passed my daughters in the den and entered the kitchen, I began to cry uncontrollably. I dropped my purse, phone, and keys as I fell to the kitchen floor. I completely broke down at the thought of this whole mess playing out. I will never forget my older daughter coming into the kitchen and asking me, "Mommy, are you okay?" As she rubbed my shoulder, she calmly said, "It's going to be alright." I told her that I was alright and supposed to be meeting with my ex, but I didn't have the strength to see him today. When I looked into her eyes, I was embarrassed. I had shown her just how broken I had become because of one person. It was then that I picked up some of my belongings and retreated to my bedroom to lie down for a while. As I was resting, she actually spoke with my ex over the phone. I'm not sure exactly what she said to him, but I do know that she made it clear that she didn't like how he had treated me and that it was best that he stay away from me.

If we knew from the very first moment that we met someone that they were not the right person for us, we would save so much time, energy, money, dignity, and effort. If we knew the exact day and time that we were going to meet our husband, we could plan our lives accordingly and just enjoy life until that designated time. In actuality, both of the previous statements are true. There is a set time and place for both of you to meet, and God lets us know if someone we are potentially interested in or are currently entertaining is not right for us. However, it takes a huge amount of faith to be patient while God's work is completed. Most of us do not have that type of faith and believe me when I say that I am the first one to raise my hand in this department. My faith has been very shallow when concerning relationships; I have always assisted God. Since my last relationship and the beginning of my "husband journal," I have learned to rest in God's assurance that my husband is on his way. God has shown me how to relax and enjoy my life in the process. Now don't get me wrong, with every room I enter, I immediately begin to wonder if my husband is there waiting to bump into me. With every place that I go, I wonder if today will be the day. That is not a lack of faith that is expectancy. There is a huge difference.

Think about this analogy of faith and expectancy. If you've ever been pregnant, in the beginning, you aren't completely sure that you are pregnant. You have to trust the pregnancy test, or you trust the doctor's word. You feel slightly hormonal and you show some signs of being pregnant. As you begin to tell people around you about the pregnancy, neither of you can see it because you aren't showing and there is no actual baby yet. So you trust and believe that at the end of nine months, you will have a healthy baby boy or girl. As each day gets closer to your due date, you are expecting the arrival at any moment. You walk around thinking, "Will this be the day? Will I meet my son or daughter today?" You know the day is coming (faith), and it will be wonderful; you just don't know exactly when it will happen (expectancy).

So for me, I know my husband is on his way, and I walk with expectancy thinking "Will this be the day? Will I meet my husband today?" I don't stress the process anymore. That's how I got into this whole mess. I still get lonely and wish I had someone in my life, but the alternative of trying to control my own destiny has proven to be too hurtful and damaging for me. My advice is to just take each day as it comes. We can enjoy our lives as they are and live in the moment, but we can also rejoice in the fact that today we might meet our husband.

In God's Workshop

"In those days I, Daniel, was mourning three full weeks. I ate no pleasant food, no meat or wine came into my mouth, nor did I anoint myself at all, till three whole weeks were fulfilled."
~ Daniel 10:2 – 3.

After my relationship ended, I hit a brick wall and felt even more worthless than ever. I knew without a doubt that I wasn't supposed to be with him anymore. I heard that message loud and clear. Yet the verbal and emotional abuse left me in ruins. I looked at the pictures we took, and I could see the secret pain that my smile hid. Every picture reminded me of something that he and I did or a moment we shared together. There were both good and bad times, but then I would quickly recall the circumstances that surrounded each picture. Either we had just gotten back together after a nasty argument, or we were on the brink of an argument. There was a back story to every photo. Each three to five second a picture represented only a fraction of my life. In reality, I was living on egg shells in my relationship with him. I didn't know how to even talk to him at times because I was afraid that he would blow up at me. He was so verbally volatile at times that all I could do was cry when he spoke to me. I blamed myself for his anger. Why couldn't I just stop making him mad at me?

As I sat one night on the sofa watching an episode of "What Would You Do?" one of the segments was about an abused woman. The scenario took place inside of a flea market. The actors played husband and wife, and the husband character began to verbally belittle the wife as passersby overheard his comments. The camera captured people's responses to their scene as they watched from a distance, and how these people put themselves in a potentially dangerous situation to save a seemingly abused woman. In each scene, there was at least one courageous person who intervened to stop this woman from leaving with that man.

As he hurled insults at her, tears welled in my eyes. His words and her reaction immediately struck a chord in me. I watched his body language as the hair on my arms raised, and my heart pounded in my chest. It was as if I was hearing those words through my ex's mouth. My mind flashed back to the morning when he and I were in a home improvement store picking up gardening supplies. We had just gotten into a heated argument the night before that dragged into that morning. The woman's facial expression reminded me of how I felt that day as he stood over me in the store. As I was standing in the aisle in tears, I was trembling and wishing that someone would say something to stop what was happening. As he spoke to me that day, his eyes were cold and void of human expression. I won't go into detail about everything that happened throughout that day, but I will say that it was the day I felt like the verbal abuse almost transitioned into physical abuse.

How did I get so low? I used to be a very strong, independent woman who set a good example for her kids. How did I allow someone who brought absolutely nothing to the table to talk to me in such a way that it almost destroyed me? The toxicity and memories of that relationship left me unable to eat or drink. I had become thin, frail, and out of shape. I was spiraling into a deep depression, and all my hair had turned grey on one side of my head. My eyes were just dark, lifeless pools. I could barely smile or laugh because the weight of all I had been through was wearing me out. I looked around and everything that I worked so hard for was falling apart. My career was hanging on by a thread, my dissertation was not finished, and I was struggling to get by life back on track with God. The only thing that I could think to do was drink to relieve the pain. I would sit on my sofa in the evenings and drink either an entire bottle of wine or glasses Jack Daniels Honey™ on the rocks until I passed out. I was quickly approaching the brink of alcoholism. I spent a lot of time alone thinking about how everything played out and drinking drowned out those memories. Why did I allow this person to drag me down to this point? Why did this relationship change me so much?

My student had given me a flyer for his church in Decatur. So one Sunday my daughters and I woke up, got dressed, and headed to his church. The service was phenomenal. The entire congregation welcomed us with open arms. In particular, I took a special liking to his mother. She is the church mother. She walked right up to me on the first day and hugged me. Her embrace was comforting. Without words, it let me know that I was in the right place and that everything was going to be alright. She told me that she's my mother now and that we needed to exchange numbers before I left. As service began, I felt the anointing of the Holy Spirit throughout that building. Both he and his wife laid hands on me and prayed with me. As she pressed into my stomach and prayed in tongues, I could feel a weight being lifted off me. After a few weeks of attending, he walked up to me during service and gave me a high five. He told me "You are surviving your season! The residue from what you experienced will not haunt you. You will look back and think WOW, I went through that?" I thought to myself, not only am I surviving my season; I am thriving in my season! I had committed to not only getting better but to being fully healed from all the pain I had experienced. I joined their church a month after I began attending.

On August 1, 2016, God placed it in my spirit to begin another Daniel fast. He told me that I needed time to be under His care or as I like to call it, "In God's Workshop." So I began my second longest fast of my life, thus far. I woke up, and I deactivated my Facebook and Instagram accounts. With the time that I would normally spend on social media, I began reading and studying my Bible. I cut out all meats, sweets, alcohol, and bread from my diet. I entered this fast determined to purge all the ugliness from my relationships out of my life. I promised God that I would not let Him go until I felt better, and I would not allow Satan to destroy my life any longer. Each day, I entrenched myself in God's Word because I was not giving up until I felt relief. As I wrote this section of this book, I was on day 26 of my fast. During this fast, the Holy Spirit has spoken to me numerous times. He has broken the spiritual ties that were preventing me from getting over my ex. He has freed me from the bondage of my past. Most importantly, He gave me the words to put in this book. God told me that by releasing my story, it would give me the completed peace and restoration that I needed to heal.

One of the important things that my student mentioned to me while he was prophesying back in June was that I needed to ask God for a spiritual divorce from my ex. I needed to sever the spiritual connection that was trying to draw me back to him and causing me so much heartache. I believe fasting is one way to separate yourself from everyone and everything going on around you. It is a time for you to focus on God and His healing. So I pressed on for initially 21 days, but it turned into 30 days. I deleted old text messages, pictures, voicemail messages, and threw away everything that he'd ever given me. It wasn't much, so that part was easy. I begged God to forgive me for ignoring His warnings and for being disobedient. I set aside all of my pride and laid flat on my face before God to ask Him for forgiveness. It's not until you get to your lowest point in life that you realize how you are destroying it. By "playing

God or matchmaker" in our own lives, we perpetuate sin and every single ugly thing that comes with it.

I am a beautiful, vibrant, intelligent young woman who has a lot to offer any man that is interested in dating me. I do not have to settle for less or allow someone to treat me with total disregard for my feelings and with complete disrespect.

During one of my recent conversations with my pastor's mother, I began to reveal to her the vision that God had given me about this book. She was completely captivated by my story about my late husband and the night that he passed way. After I explained each detail of the story, she told me that I needed to finish writing this book. I told her that the pain and resentment built up from my experience with my ex was holding me back from writing. I did not want him to be the focal point of my story. I swore to her that I did not want to carry the pain of that relationship into any other parts of my life. I knew that God would not allow me to meet my husband if I was still so damaged. I also shared with her that I was still on a fast, and she asked what day I was on. At the time it was day 25, I told her that I began with a 21 day fast, but I felt that God had not released me yet so I was pressing on until He did. She said that only once in her life had she gone on a 30 day fast, but on that fast God accelerates healing, breaks spiritual bondage, and restores you.

If you chose to include fasting as part of your spiritual healing, I recommend doing some research on it first. I also recommend speaking with a minister or pastor to find out more about what you will experience on your fast. While you are on a fast, you are under God's special covering and protection because spiritual warfare is going on around you. God will reveal special things to you that you might normally ignore or be oblivious to understanding. During my time on that fast, God showed me things about my ex-boyfriend that I did not share with anyone other than my pastor's mother. He also reassured me that He has a wonderful husband for me. He poured such love and affection into my spirit as I studied and read His Word.

After I got off the phone with my pastor's mother, God pressed even harder for me to write my story. He would wake me up at odd hours in the morning during my fast. He revealed to me that as I wrote my story, those wounds would begin to heal. The important thing I want to share in this chapter is not necessarily about fasting. It is about entering "God's Workshop" so that He can work on you and so that you can heal. We are all carrying baggage from old relationships. Those wounds take time to heal. Often, we jump from one relationship into another without taking a breather. There is saying that goes like this, "It takes a man to get over a man." This couldn't be further from the truth. It takes God to get over a man. You need to spend time with God to heal before you can enter a new relationship otherwise, you will continue cycling in stage two of your trial. You will never get to the third stage and be *"perfect and complete, lacking nothing"* as mentioned in *James 1:4 NKJV*. Let God have this time! I don't know if fasting social media or a Daniel fast is the answer for you. I do know that you will not move forward until you devote time to heal. Find a church, pray, read the Word, seek Christian counseling, and get as close to God as possible so that He can mend those wounds. In His Workshop is where all of those past relationship and spiritual ties can be broken.

The Husband Journal

After my encounter with God in January 2016, I began writing my second book. It explains in more detail about the night my husband died and many of the relationships that I experienced afterward. I also began journaling more, which had stopped when my ex was in the picture. I always felt like I never had anything positive to say while I was in that relationship. Most of my writing was filled with complaints about things that I had found out about him or my sheer frustration about my situation. The lies, cheating, arguing, and his constant keeping up with ex-girlfriends had taken a toll on me. Those closest to me could see that I wasn't myself anymore. I was becoming more and more like him every day. I had become reclusive or I would take my anger out on those around me. Well, as I started journaling again, it was my way to repair my brokenness.

During our break-up in January, God placed it on my heart to start a very special journal. So in February, after I ended the 21 days Daniel fast, I began writing to a very special person.

God told me to write a *"Husband Journal."* I've only shared this vision with a few people until now. My first entry in this journal was:

"Dear Future husband,

When you read this journal, I want you to know that I did the work needed to become whole so that I could be your wife. It was not easy, but I committed my life to you long before we were together. On days when you are angry with me, read this journal. On days that you love me, read this journal. On both of those days, realize how much you mean to me and how I never want to give up on our love. This book is my first commitment to you."

When my ex texted me on Valentine's Day and we reconnected, I stop journaling again. But my mind kept lingering back to the things I wrote and the person that I was writing to. I realized that the person that I was with and the person that I was writing to were completely different. One thing that I caution you not to do is "do not stop writing to your future husband." At the time that I was back with my ex, I would look over on my book shelf at my journal and feel ashamed. For the most part, I knew the person in that journal that I was writing to was not the person that I was actually in a relationship with. The man I wanted loved God. He was a man of integrity, honesty, and he was good to me. It was as though I was with his polar opposite. I think to myself now that journaling is another sign from God to help us evaluate whether we are dealing with someone that is ordained by Him. In my other relationships, I did not get the same warning signs that I got in with my ex-boyfriend. Some of the signs came in the form of a hunch, or intuition, or that small, still voice that we all hear. When you aren't sure if you are hearing the word of God or not, that makes it hard to decide whether you're giving up on someone that you're supposed to be with or not. I can't tell you how to hear the Holy Spirit in your current situation. All I know is that if you call on Him, He will answer you. And if what you write down is completely different from what you're dealing with, then it may be time to reevaluate your situation.

Three profound verses come to my mind when I think of my *"Husband Journal."* The first is *Habakkuk 2:3 "Write the vision and make it plain on tablets, that he may run who reads it. For the vision is yet for an appointed time; but at the end it will speak, and it will not lie. Though it tarries, wait for it; because it will surely come, it will not tarry."* When you really think about this verse, it is mind blowing. First, God charges us to write down our thoughts because, our thoughts become our words, and our words become our actions. Listen, when you write in your *Husband Journal*, you need to be specific. Yes, I had my husband list, but I felt like something was missing. It didn't keep me connected to my husband on a daily basis. I needed to be able to speak to him in the spirit, and I needed something to keep me focused on the future and not the past. Speak to that person as though they are already in your life because they will be at the appointed time. You need to speak into existence things that you want for your marriage. If you want flowers and romantic walks in the park, begin thanking him for that. If you want to be shown affection on a daily basis, thank him in advance for all those special moments. If you love his cooking, tell him now. Thank him for each and everything imaginable. And if you run out of things to say, start all over again with thanking him.

When I first wrote to my husband, I wasn't fully committed to the idea. I thought it was kind of dumb and impersonal. I mean who writes to some fictional person that may or may not ever appear? But God showed me that I was speaking as though that person is already in my life because, in actuality, he is. He has already been chosen specifically for me. Although I don't know exactly what he looks like, I know what his spirit is like. That's easy to write to because it matches mine. He is the other part of me. God created both of us with the other in mind. He knows what strengths we each bring to the table, as well as He knows our weaknesses. He knows how we will compensate for one another's weaknesses. What you write will be the truth about your husband, so you need to speak life and positivity into your spouse. Encourage him throughout your journal. Keep him as motivated and focused as you are.

You also have to remember that God tells us that they will surely come. This means that He has not forgotten YOU! We are assured to do something or to get something if we write it down. If you can visualize it, then something happens in your mind. It's like it alters your perception of things making it into your reality. For me, my *"Husband Journal"* not only helps me focus on my future, but it puts a real person in place. I am speaking to my future husband. Someday he will read the words that I have written because this journal is designed to be his wedding gift. Yes! Isn't that a beautiful gift? Besides the gift of being able to call you his wife on your wedding day, your husband will know your thoughts about him before the two of you married. He will know how much you loved him. He will know your dedication, sacrifice, and unyielding faith in God. He will know anything that you chose to share with him.

As I mentioned earlier, when I began my husband journal, I was vague. I addressed him as my "future husband." As time went on I realized that he's not my "future husband," he is my "husband." He exists right now. We are already married in God's eyes in the spirit. If that doesn't put it in perspective, then I don't know what will. You can go ahead and call him a pet name if you'd like. Whatever you feel comfortable with saying, write it down! After my last round with my ex, I was focused like a laser with my writing. I knew exactly what I wanted to speak into my husband. So when I joke about not going out on a second date with the guy who wouldn't pray over dinner, it's not to mock him. It's to say that I am being specific Lord. I need a husband who prays. He will need to show me in some shape, form, or fashion that prayer is part of his life for me to know this is ordained by you. If he cannot do that, I'm taking that as a sign, and I refuse to settle for anyone who does not pray because I saw where that led me last time.

Now that we know God's promise to us, and we know that it requires faith. How do we activate our faith? *"What good does it, dear brothers and sisters, if you say you have faith but don't show it by your actions? Can that kind of faith save anyone?" James 2:14 NLT.* This verse tells us that faith without works is dead. Your *"Husband Journal"* is the work that you are putting in place to show God that you believe His promise to you. It is twofold. You are not only activating your faith through writing, but you are activating God. You are putting the ball in His court. You are saying to God, "Hey, you promised me something wonderful and I trust you to deliver it. I know that you aren't going to give me any junk. You wouldn't do that to me because I'm your child. I am no longer going to use my own effort to get a husband. I give that full responsibility over to you, Lord. And when it's time, I will get exactly what you promised or better". Every time you put that pen to paper, you are activating your faith in His promise. Now I'm not saying that you become a recluse and only journal in a book to find your mate. You will need to do the other things that God places on your heart to do. But journaling is one way to stay focused, and you are sowing into His promise.

The next verse that comes to mind is *Matthew 9:28 – 30* *"And Jesus said to them, 'Do you believe that I am able to do this?' They said to Him, 'Yes, Lord.' Then He touched their eyes, saying 'According to your faith let it be done to you.' And their sight was restored." – NIV.* In the first part of this verse, Jesus asked the blind men if they believe that He is able to heal them. I have to ask myself this question repeatedly. I am human, so I do have doubts. All the pain from the past likes to creep up into my mind and cause me to doubt God. That's when I write. I have to show Satan that God has not forgotten me. The second part of this verse tells us that it is according to our faith that we receive healing. During my first encounter with God, He told me that He has a good husband for me. He told me that my husband would help me and not harm me. There is no doubt in my mind about that, but I let my fears take hold of that promise. So God did His part in revealing His promise, but I choose not to believe His word. So according to my faith at the time, which was none, I kept receiving a very different gift. I got exactly what my fears manifested which was verbal abuse and a path headed to destruction.

The beautiful thing that I have experienced about this *"Husband Journal"* is that I feel like I am speaking directly to my husband. I share with him my daily thoughts, fears, faith, adventures, spiritual journey, and he knows that I am writing this book about him. When we meet, I will still be journaling about our first date, our first kiss, and our plans for marriage. The culmination of all my experiences on the journey to becoming his wife will be documented. He can read it over and over again to see exactly how much I love him, how I waited on him, and how much faith I have in God to bring us together. I encourage everyone reading this book, male or female, to activate their faith. Begin writing to your future spouse. It is the best, most intimate gift you can give them.

Dear Husband

"But the Lord said to him, 'Go for he is a chosen vessel of Mine to bear My name before Gentiles, kings, and the children of Israel. For I will show him how many things he must suffer for My name's sake'" ~ Acts 9:15 – 16 NKJV.

I'm not sure what my husband's name is, but I know many of the character traits and qualities that he will have. Often when I am studying my Bible, God will bring to my attention the names of so many valiant men in the Bible. When we think of King David, King Solomon, Abraham, or Isaac, we know each of their roles throughout Biblical history. We read about their purpose in God's plan, and we also see their fallibility. For example, David had Bathsheba's husband killed so that he could sleep with her.

In the Biblical sense, when most women think of their ideal husband, they think of Boaz. He is described in the Bible as a man of great wealth. He finds Ruth working in his fields and was drawn to her. He knew immediately that he wants her as his wife, and we are left with the "happily ever after" feeling about her story. Through her faithfulness and unyielding love of Naomi, she was in the right place for Boaz to notice her. The vindication for her loss of her husband and suffering was that God allowed her to be part of the lineage of King David and eventually Jesus Christ. The Holy Spirit showed me during one of my conversations in my prayer closet that my husband will find me just as Boaz found Ruth. He will know that he is my husband before I even notice him. My husband is a Christian, and his heart pursues God. He possesses the traits and values that I am seeking. God knows exactly what I need, and has ordained a specific individual to fulfill that role in my life.

One of the men in the Bible that I have studied extensively is Paul. As I began to read about Paul in the Bible, I realized that he was a despicable person at first. When he was Saul, he persecuted Christians for a long time before he was saved. *"Then Saul, still breathing threats and murder against the disciples of the Lord, went to the high priest and asked letters from him to the synagogues of Damascus, so that if he found any who were of the Way, whether men or women, he might bring them bound to Jerusalem" ~ Acts 9: 1 NKJV.* On his way to Damascus, the spirit of the Jesus stopped him and asked, *"Saul, Saul, why are you persecuting Me?"* After Saul spent three days in blindness and without anything to eat or drink, God sent Ananias to lay hands on him. God described Saul to Ananias as *"But the Lord said to him, 'Go for he is a chosen vessel of Mine to bear My name before Gentiles, kings, and the children of Israel"* Acts 9:15 NKJV. After Ananias laid hands on a blinded Saul, he was transform into the Apostle Paul.

Saul is the perfect example of what we do not want in a husband. He despised God with all his heart. He was on a personal crusade to kill all Christians, but once God changed him, it was as though Paul was a completely different person from Saul. He did not know it, but he was God's chosen vessel. As a result, when we read throughout the New Testament, we constantly hear Paul's name. *"God did extraordinary miracles through Paul, so that even handkerchiefs and aprons that had touched him were taken to the sick, and their illnesses were cured and the evil spirits left them."* ~ *Acts 19:11-12 NIV.* Paul became an integral part of God's plan to the extent that the Jews could not understand his power. Many of them tried to duplicate his ability to cast out demons and to heal the sick but were unable to do so. Paul suffered throughout his life for Christ. Much of the same persecution he inflicted on Christians was inflicted upon him. I could go on and on about Paul because he accomplished so many things in his life although his beginning was less than stellar.

The significance of this story and the comparison of Paul is that our future husband's life will not be perfect. His past might be just as marred as ours. He has probably spent time in "God's Workshop" working out past relationship and problems in life, but he is chosen by God. His purpose may not be in ministry, but our future husband does have a purpose. God has shown me that my husband is a man of God. He has been chosen as a vessel to serve God, but before his calling, he may have been similar to Saul. God has been working on my husband for many, many years. He has a story to tell, just as I do. His journey, life experiences, and pain were all to create a better man, father, and leader in him. I do not slight him for his experiences because I understand God's purpose. In actuality, Paul is within all of us. We have so many issues, baggage, and ugliness in our lives that we think we are beyond God's forgiveness. We feel as though God cannot use us.

The things that I write about are specific and speak about the character of my husband, but they are also about me. Because this is a journey, I have to grow and change to meet the standards that I am setting. My husband is just as determined as I am not to settle for less than God has promised him. So I must get myself right for our appointed time to meet. A God ordained marriage is going to require a better version of you. Here are some tips to work on while waiting.

Focus on your character:

1. Put God first. This might require some time alone with God. It will also require more time with God through reading and studying His Word. – *2 Corinthians 8:5*

2. Your body is a vessel of God. You cannot allow sex to cloud your judgment about men. Get rid of old phone numbers, pictures, and other reminders that keep haunting you. If these reminders are causing confusion in your life and drawing you back to exes, get rid of them immediately. Holding on to those things allows the past to remain in the present, which possibly delays your future. It is up to you to stop repeating the second phase or the test of life, so take serious action. – *Corinthians 6:19; Matthew 7:6*

3. Ask God for a spiritual divorce from past relationships. The sooner you break those spiritual bonds, the better you will feel. Let go the thoughts and ideas about your ex. Break the strongholds that want to keep you in that relationship. – *Isaiah 58: 6-11*

4. Pray often and without ceasing. As a matter of fact, become a prayer warrior because this battle is not physical but spiritual – *Ephesians 6:12*

5. Fast. If this is your first time, seek Christian counsel on how to fast. Start with something small like one meal or social media. Fully commit to completing your fast so that you can hear from God and grow closer to Him. I recommend the *21 Day Daniel Fast* if you have some experience in fasting. You can extend it to 30 days as I did if you feel God pressing you to continue in the fast. – *Daniel 10:3; Isaiah 58*

6. Forgive yourself. God gives us new mercy every single day. Ask His forgiveness for your past mistakes and disobedience. He will heal your wounds. – *Psalm 130*

7. Forgive men from past relationships. Commit to letting it go. As long as you harbor unforgiveness and hatred, you block God's blessing. Do not carry that baggage into your marriage. Realize that much of it was necessary so that you can be in the place to receive God's best for your life. – Lu*ke 17:4; Philippians 1:6*

8. Submit to your husband. You have to set aside your pride and allow your husband to take his role in your

marriage. A God ordained husband knows how to be a leader, protector, and provider. He will not abuse his role or misuse your submission. – *Ephesians 5:22, 24*

9. Vow to be a peacemaker. Learn to resolve issues quickly, so those issues do not create confusion in your household. – *Philippians 4:7;John 16:33; Thessalonians 3:16;Matthew 5:9; James 3:18*

10. Remember that you are valuable. A woman is precious in God's sight. Don't ever devalue yourself in any way. – *Psalm 45:5*

11. Practice listening to God's voice. Be silent and still before God. Give yourself time alone with Him so that you can learn the sound of His voice. The more time you spend with Him, the more familiar you will become with His voice. – *Psalm 85:8; John 10:27-29*

12. Praise God NOW for your husband. Begin thanking and praising God because your husband is on his way! – *Psalm 150*

13. Don't settle for anything less than the best. Loneliness will make you settle for things and people that are not meant for you. Usually, you feel the loneliest when you are closest to meeting your God ordained husband.

14. Guard your heart. Satan knows how close you are to meeting your husband, so he will send a decoy. Do not give your heart away without closely examining this new man's intentions. If he is pressuring you to sleep with him or becomes a huge distraction from all of your progress, let him go. – *Proverbs 4:23*

15. Ask God to restore your trust in men. All men are not the same. You cannot judge all of them based on your personal experiences. God's selection for you will be different than what you have experienced in the past. – *Psalm 20:7, Psalm 31:14; Psalm 56:11*

16. Seek Christian counseling to help discuss the issues that you are experiencing while healing. It's going to be a tough road, so you need someone to talk to that will give you sound advice.

17. Get involved in a Bible based church. Go to church and get active. One of the best ways to spend your spare time is working for God.

18. Journal! Write down your feelings so that you can process them. If you are feeling happy or sad, write that down. Keep track of your progress.

Once you've done the work on your life, it's time to ask God for what you want. Since God is not going to give you anything less than you deserve, give it some thought and be specific. My expectations might be different from yours in what you need in a husband, but here are some suggestions when you begin to write.

Focus on his character:

1. He should be a Christian. – *Psalm 34*

2. He should be a man of integrity. – *Titus 2:7; Proverbs 11:3*

3. He should be faithful to your marriage vows. – *Malachi 2:15*

4. He should see you as his rib/partner. – *Genesis 2:21-24*

5. He should love you as Christ loves the church. – *Ephesians 5:25, 28-29*

6. He should have godly goals. – *2 Peter 1:5-8*

7. He should be a leader/head of the household. – *Ephesians 5:22-24; Colossians 3:18; I Peter 3:1*

8. He should be a provider. – *Proverbs 13:22*

9. He should be an example to his friends and family. – *Jeremiah 32:40-41; 2 Corinthians 1:12*

10. He honors and respects his mother and father. – *Ephesians 6:2; Exodus 20:12; Deuteronomy 5:16*

11. He should have a prayer life. – *Matthew 21:22; James 5:16*

12. He should have good fruit on his tree. – *Matthew 7:16-20; Ezekiel 14:12*

13. He is willing to put his marriage first. – *Ephesians 5:31*

14. He tells the truth. A man of honor will tell the truth even in the most difficult circumstances. He will not be double-minded or present a lot of double-talk. – *James 1:8*

15. He is a man of action. He is more focused on proving himself with his actions than he is with words. As a matter of fact, he might be a man of few words and much action. – *Jeremiah 32: 39*

Conclusion

God has been pressing me to write as part of my healing for a very long time. I have struggled with writing this book because I didn't know how my story would be received. When you have been verbally or physically abused, it damages your soul. You begin to question yourself-worth. Doubt, self-loathing, and fear overtake your thoughts and actions. I have struggled with this book because I didn't want to be viewed a gripe session about my ex-boyfriend or revenge for the end of our relationship. It's quite the contrary; he is not the focal point but a catalyst. This book is part of my healing, but it is also a way for other women to heal. I spent an afternoon talking with one of my closest friends about what happened in my relationship. She could relate because she had been through something similar with her ex-husband. She was able to admit that "she is an abused woman." Her words made me realize that so many women hide behind this stigma.

As beautiful women of God, we waste so much of our time entertain men who are not Christians, who are not willing to marry us, and who are not ordained as our husbands. We throw away our pearls to swine because we do not listen to the discernment of God. We accept abuse, lies, deceit as part of the journey in a relationship. If you are in an abusive relationship, I ask that you seek help immediately. Even verbal abuse is still abuse.

While writing this book, I realized how much God prepared me for my experience and protected me from being harmed. He began to bring to my remembrance all the special Bible verses that He has given me over the years. When I pieced them together while writing, it seemed effortless. God has been placing parts of this book in my soul for years. Many of those Bible verses have been kept in a frame in my bathroom, and all of the other verses are ones that He led me to as I wrote. Beautiful woman of God, remember that God's hand is always with you. He is guiding you through your experience. You must listen to His voice. I wholeheartedly admit that refusing to listen was my biggest mistake. I kept trying to fix something that was clearly not ordained by God. I chose to stay after God warned me and sent numerous signs. Although I directly disobeyed God, He protected me. I now realize that the outcome of that relationship could have been horrific. The most important thing that I gained from this experience is how to listen to the Holy Spirit. God speaks to each of us differently. It may not come in the form of a man of God prophesying to you in a classroom, it may not come in a prayer closet through the Holy Spirit, but it WILL COME. If you **ask** God to show you, He will **answer**. You just have to be willing to obey His commands. The hardest thing I had to do in this situation was obey God's Word. I walked away from a situation without knowing all of the underlying details. It wasn't until later that God revealed the lies, cheating, and deception. Much of it has been revealed as I am writing this book. So the raw emotions that you feel while reading are real. My pain is real, and my journey is real. I am still working on forgiveness because my love for him was so deep, but every day I thank God for delivering me out of that situation. The forgiveness and healing will come in due time. I have no doubt. God has already shown me that I have a beautiful life on the other side of this experience. So He will definitely repay me double for my trouble and give me beauty for my ashes.

"He changes the times and the seasons; He removes kings and sets up kings. He gives wisdom to the wise and knowledge to those who have understanding!" ~ Daniel 2:21 AMP. God's promise is clear to me, and He has the ability to change things very quickly in our lives. He is able to change my situation in an instant. The first part of this verse reminds me that although I had a man in my life, as I entered into a new season, he was removed QUICKLY. God removed someone that was unhealthy for me to set up my king. God has also given me the wisdom to understand what happened and its purpose in my life. Just one year ago, I thought the person that I was in a relationship with was going to be my husband. I thought if I prayed enough and asked God to help us, we could make it through our problems. But God's plan is much different than my plan. He can see what I would have been dealing with in

the future had I stayed with that man. We have to count it as joy when God removes certain people out of our lives for good.

The healing, faith, discerning God's voice, and manifestation of His promises are the central points of this book. God has used me as His vessel and to share my story. I have no doubt that everything that I've gone through is to help someone else. I know that my experiences with love, abuse, loss, and heartbreak are not uncommon. As I am writing this book, I am still continuing on my journey in God's workshop. Most importantly, I am still waiting on my husband, but this time I am fully relying on God. I am lead by His voice and spiritual discernment. I know that thorough journaling to my husband; He is establishing my king to take his rightful place in my life.

In conclusion, I know one specific question has arisen for many of you reading this book, which is 'How can you write about something that hasn't even been proven yet? How do I know if my husband really exists and if you will ever meet him?" The truth is that I reread this book all the time, I look at my journal, and I pray constantly. The small still voice that I have in my spirit lets me know that I am correct. Remember that God told me that He hasn't forgotten me, so I know this will manifest. But it's now up to God to make this work. I have done my part. I exercised my faith, and now it's in God's Hands.

31 Day Devotional for Journaling to Your Future Husband

Day 1

Dear future husband,

Today is a new beginning in God's journey for our lives. This is the day that I place my destiny in God's hands. I surrender my way of doing things to Him.

Thoughts:

Today is a fresh start. Give your old habits of dating over to God.

Verses:

Isaiah 43: 18-19; 2 Corinthians 5:17

31 Day Devotional for Journaling to Your Future Husband

Day 2

Dear future husband,

God's plan for us is greater than we could ever imagine. We are His children and deserve the very best. All things work together for the good of those that love God.

Thoughts:

All the hurt and pain of the past have led to this point. God will use it for His glory.

Verse:

Romans 8:28

31 Day Devotional for Journaling to Your Future Husband

Day 3

Dear future husband,

As I waiting on God's appointed time for us to meet, I rededicate my body to Him. I am a vessel of God. With this sacrifice and commitment, I am giving up another area of control and bad decision making in my life.

Thoughts:

Surrendering this journey to God also means surrendering your body. Celibacy is part of the dedication and belief that God has something much greater for you. Remember that your way of doing things hasn't worked and you keep getting the same results. It's time to try something new. Celibacy helps you stay focused and to wait on God.

Verse:

I Corinthians 6:19

31 Day Devotional for Journaling to Your Future Husband

Day 4

Dear future husband,

I know that you are on the other side of this journey. I know that you are experiencing the same ups and downs. Don't let those trials deter your faith in God. He is mightier than any obstacles we face. He has promised us that He will never leave or forsake us.

Thoughts:

Think about what led you to this journey. Maybe it was a bad break-up or a series of bad choices. Those challenges don't go away because you are trying something different. They actually get harder, but keep pressing forward and believing that God has something good for you waiting on the other end. Now faith is the substance of things hoped for, the evidence of things not seen.

Verse:

Hebrew 11:1

31 Day Devotional for Journaling to Your Future Husband

Day 5

Dear future husband,

Today I want you to know that I love you. I appreciate the strong man of God that you are and all the sacrifices you have made to become closer with God. I pray for a continuing hedge of protection around you as you travel through life today.

Thoughts:

Spend time in prayer today. Ask God to cover and to protect your husband. Begin to intercede on his behalf. Your prayers strengthen and encourage his spirit. Prayer is one of the greatest forms of love in a relationship.

Verse:

Romans 15:30

31 Day Devotional for Journaling to Your Future Husband

Day 6

Dear future husband,

Since we are already one in the spirit, which means we are equally yoked. God has matched us according to His design and purpose for our lives. I know that God will not bring anyone into my life that is not here to make my life better and to bring me closer to Him.

Thoughts:

You are a child of God. He does not give His children anything less than the best. That means you and your future husband are equally yoked. Don't settle for something less than what God has promised you because you are lonely or feel like it's taking too long. It's not your job to convince some to go to church or to have a relationship with God.

Verse:

II Corinthians 6:14

31 Day Devotional for Journaling to Your Future Husband

Day 7

Dear future husband,

Today I am asking God to grant me a spiritual divorce from past relationships, hurt, anger, pain, bitterness, suffering, failure, and rejection. I am asking God to restore my love and faith in men. I will not allow my past to hinder my future with you.

Thoughts:

You cannot enter into a new relationship carrying the scars from old relationships. Ask God to grant you a spiritual divorce from your past. This includes former boyfriends. Sever those ties that will hold you back from loving the right man. Stop communicating with your exes because you are lonely. Whether you know it or not, those spiritual bonds harden your heart and spirit. They cause you to repeat the same mistakes over and over again because you have not broken them. Ask God for forgiveness and deliverance.

Verse:

Isaiah 58: 6-11

31 Day Devotional for Journaling to Your Future Husband

Day 8

Dear future husband,

Today I thank you being a man of God, a provider, a leader, the cornerstone of our family, and an example of how a man should treat his wife. As you are the head of this household, God is the head of your life.

Thoughts:

God will send someone that has the qualities needed to be the head of a household. One of the most identifiable quality is how he treats you. He will not send someone that will disrespect, abuse, or mistreat you in any away. He is sending someone that will love you like Christ loves the church.

Verses:

I Corinthians 11:3; Ephesians 5:23-28

31 Day Devotional for Journaling to Your Future Husband

Day 9

Dear future husband,

God has promised in His perfect plan that we are to be united. Our unity is already written in His Word, in our hearts, and in the spirit. Before we were born, God placed His purpose and destiny in each of us so it must come to fruition.

Thoughts:

God has placed the desire to be a wife in your heart for a reason. That desire was created because He matched you with your husband long before you knew of your own existence. We were not created to independent of one another. Allow God to use that desire to guide you to the person He has chosen for you.

Verse:

I Corinthians 11:11-12

31 Day Devotional for Journaling to Your Future Husband

Day 10

Dear future husband,

You are valuable in my eyes. I see your worth! You were hand chosen by God to be my husband for a specific reason. You are special to Him and to me. As you go throughout your day, the world may try to tear you down, but I am here to lift you up.

Thoughts:

Let him know his worth. The world is designed to break him so speak words of encouragement over your future husband today. He needs to hear those positive words of affirmation from you to strengthen him and to build his confidence. Those special words are more important than anything else in his life.

Verse:

Hebrews 3:13

31 Day Devotional for Journaling to Your Future Husband

Day 11

Dear future husband,

I thank you for being such a hard worker and provider for this family. I pray that God blesses you with increase in your life. I pray over your finances and the fruits of your labor. May you be prosperous and multiply in all areas of your life. Your life is full of open doors and endless possibilities in the name of Jesus!

Thoughts:

Ask God to bless your husband today. Pray over his endeavors and that he will have future success in his life. The seeds that he is sowing day will reap a bountiful harvest in the future.

Verses:

Ezekiel 47: 12; Proverbs 13:22

31 Day Devotional for Journaling to Your Future Husband

Day 12

Dear future husband,

Today as the enemy tries to use depression, loneliness, and impatient as stumbling blocks on this journey I pray for our protection and that God helps us to remain focused on His promises.

Thoughts:

In times of loneliness, the enemy will have you doubt the process of waiting. He will bring temptation in every form imaginable and try to steal or delay God's gift to you. This is when you need to get on your knees and pray. Don't allow temptation to cause you to stray from your path. The enemy has no power over you! Remember to fight in the spirit daily against the enemy. He has no place in your relationship.

Verse:

Ephesians 6:12

31 Day Devotional for Journaling to Your Future Husband

Day 13

Dear future husband,

Today I keep hearing the words "in His timing". We have a special appointment with one another. We do not know the time or the place when our first encounter will occur, but we do know that it will happen. Until that day comes, remain ready and be on one accord. Continue to pray, fast, study, and read your Word so that you will be ready to meet me. Each day on this journey is bringing us closer to one another.

Thoughts:

Be ready for the day that God brings your husband into your life. Stay active in God's ministry and busy in His Word. Those are the things that will keep you aligned with God's timing.

Verses:

Habakkuk 2:3; Matthew 25: 1-13

31 Day Devotional for Journaling to Your Future Husband

Day 14

Dear future husband,

Thank you for being my partner. Thank you for treating me with the love and kindness that I deserve. On the days that I feel most vulnerable, you are by myside, and I am by yours. You always remind me that I am your rib!

Thoughts:

Not only will you recognize your husband's place in your life, but he will see yours in his life as well. He will make room for you because he values your placement in his life. He knows that you are his rib.

Verses:

Genesis 2:21-24

31 Day Devotional for Journaling to Your Future Husband

Day 15

Dear future husband,

Repeat these three words "it was necessary". Whatever you have experienced was necessary to bring us to this place of total dependence on God. Don't focus on mistakes, misfortunes, and mishaps in past relationships. Remember that everything is God's plan is necessary to redirect our paths.

Thoughts:

Even the worst experiences, relationships, and break ups are designed to remove us from something that was not meant for us. God removed it because He has something better in store, and He will see it through to the end.

Verse:

Philippians 1:6

31 Day Devotional for Journaling to Your Future Husband

Day 16

Dear future husband,

I thank you for having godly goals and for striving each day to reach those goals. You understand that these goals affect our family, finances, and future together. When we put our godly goals first, it strengthens and blesses our marriage.

Thoughts:

A successful relationship must include godly goals such as prayer, worship, devotional, and time studying God's word. Work to be consistent and achieve those goals.

Verses:

2 Peter 1:5-8

31 Day Devotional for Journaling to Your Future Husband

Day 17

Dear future husband,

I respect you! You are a man of high integrity. You are a leader and not a follower. You walk tall with you head held high because you lead by your actions and not by your words. You fulfill your promises to me and place value on keeping your word.

Thoughts:

One characteristic that defines a man of integrity is his actions. Your future husband will be a man of his word. He will be consistent with his actions because he knows this is how to build trust in your relationship. Integrity and consistency build trust!

Verses:

Titus 2:7; Proverbs 11:3

31 Day Devotional for Journaling to Your Future Husband

Day 18

Dear future husband,

Remember we serve a forgiving God, so in turn, we must be forgiving. Forgive those who have hurt and wronged us in the past so that we do not carry that baggage into our future together.

Thoughts:

One major obstacle to overcome before entering into a new relationship is letting go of the bitterness and anger from the previous relationship(s). As long as you hold onto unforgiveness, you are still giving life to that old relationship. Forgive the person who has broken your heart and betrayed you; they have no place in your new relationship. Remember that all men are not the same! God's ordained husband for you will be much different than what you have experienced in the past.

Verse:

Luke 17:4

31 Day Devotional for Journaling to Your Future Husband

Day 19

Dear future husband,

Today I thank God for peace in our lives, household, and marriage. We weather the storms of life together and realize that we are each other's companions and not enemies. We do not allow differences of opinions to fester into discord and confusion. We walk in peace and love for one another. We have peace that surpasses all understanding.

Thoughts:

Ask God to provide an extra measure of peace over your relationship with your future husband. The world we live in is designed to destroy relationships and tear marriages apart. Vow to be a peacemaker in your relationship.

Verses:

Philippians 4:7; John 16:33; 2 Thessalonians 3:16; Matthew 5:9; James 3:18

31 Day Devotional for Journaling to Your Future Husband

Day 20

Dear future husband,

Thank you for having a strong, undeniable, and unwavering prayer life. In my eyes, one of your strongest attributes is your prayer life and connection with God. You are an example to our family of how a close and intimate prayer life is abounding. Thank you for leading our family in prayer, and thank you for being my prayer partner.

Thoughts:

If he doesn't pray, he can't stay! It's that simple. If he is to lead by example, then your future husband must have an intimate connection with God. A man's true strength is exhibited when he is able to kneel before God. Partnering with him in prayer creates a tighter bond and strengthens your marriage.

Verses:

Matthew 21:22; James 5:16

31 Day Devotional for Journaling to Your Future Husband

Day 21

Dear future husband,

God has appointed you to a special position in my life. You are the head of the household. As part of honoring God, I set aside my pride and submit to you as the church submits to Christ.

Thoughts:

God appointed your husband to a position of leadership. He selected your husband because he has the ability to be a good servant, role model, and leader. Honor and respect his role as the man. Submit to his position within the marriage.

Verses:

Ephesians 5:22-24; Colossians 3:18; I Peter 3:1

31 Day Devotional for Journaling to Your Future Husband

Day 22

Dear future husband,

Today I praise God for you. Praise and thanksgiving are overflowing in my spirit. God hears my praises and is moving on our behalf. There is power in my praise!

Thoughts:

Praise keeps your spirit lifted when you are feeling low. Begin praising God now for what He's already done for you and your future husband. Thank Him for His greatness, His good, His mercy, and for His perfect plan in your lives. Give God all the credit and honor. Give God your highest and loudest praise.

Verses:

Psalm 150

31 Day Devotional for Journaling to Your Future Husband

Day 23

Dear future husband,

I thank God that we have a solid marriage. Our marriage was orchestrated by God so it is blessed. We obeyed Him, listened to Him, and waited on Him. His reward to us was a marriage that is built on Him. There is no greater foundation than Him.

Thoughts:

Your marriage is built on the strongest foundation in the world. It is built on God. So when tough times arise, and they will, remember that your foundation is as solid as a rock.

Verses:

Deuteronomy 28:3; Psalm 18:2

31 Day Devotional for Journaling to Your Future Husband

Day 24

Dear future husband,

I boldly proclaim that you are a man of godly wisdom. You seek His counsel and guidance in all areas of your life. You are quick to listen to God and slow to speak because you have a constant ear for His voice. You are willing and humble enough to obey His instructions over your life.

Thoughts:

Ask God for a husband that seeks godly wisdom, instruction, knowledge, and understanding. He should be willing to go before God with every issue, big or small. He should be a continuous pupil of God and be willing to learn the lessons that God is teaching him. Boldly proclaim that your husband is a man of godly wisdom!

Verses:

Proverbs 4:5-13

31 Day Devotional for Journaling to Your Future Husband

Day 25

Dear future husband,

Thank you for being my biggest supporter, as I am yours. You always have kind and encouraging words for me each morning. We realize how much our positive words mean to each other, so we strive to uplift one another daily.

Thoughts:

Words are powerful! Your husband should always be encouraging and generous with his compliments, and you should always speak life into him. Words in a marriage should build you up and not break you down. Start each day with something positive to say to one another.

Verses:

Proverbs 15: 1, 4; Proverbs 18:21

31 Day Devotional for Journaling to Your Future Husband

Day 26

Dear future husband,

Today I speak longevity over our marriage. We have been joined together by God both spiritually and physically. What God has joined together, let no one separate.

Thoughts:

As you think about your marriage, commit to making it work even through bad times, commit to divorce not being an option in your marriage, and commit to using God as your mediator. Begin speaking longevity and commitment over your marriage now.

Verses:

Mark 10:9; Matthew 19:6

31 Day Devotional for Journaling to Your Future Husband

Day 27

Dear future husband,

You are my protector. Thank you for checking on me throughout the day. You make sure that I am always safe and never in harm, and most importantly have you safeguarded my heart to make sure it is protected. I am safe in your loving arms.

Thoughts:

The husband that God has for you is a protector. He will always ensure that you are safe. He understands that it is his job to protect you both physically and emotionally because you are the weaker vessel. He will not do things to make you feel insecure because he knows that God is holding him accountable for your heart.

Verses:

I Peter 3:7

31 Day Devotional for Journaling to Your Future Husband

Day 28

Dear future husband,

Your life is an example of the fruits of a man who is after God's own heart. Your personality and character are made of love, joy, peace, long suffering, gentleness, goodness, faith, meekness, and temperance.

Thoughts:

The fruit on a person's tree will tell you all that you need to know about them. As a Christian man, your future husband should have all of these fruits on his tree. His character should glorify God.

Verses:

Galatians 5: 22-23

31 Day Devotional for Journaling to Your Future Husband

Day 29

Dear future husband,

Thank you for being considerate, selfless, and attentive to my needs in this marriage. We equally cater to each other so that we both are satisfied and fulfilled. We realize that we were brought together to care for each other.

Thoughts:

One thing that can quickly destroy a relationship, even one ordained by God, is selfishness. Invest time in doing one another's favorite activities together.

Verses:

Philippians 2:3-4; James 3:16

31 Day Devotional for Journaling to Your Future Husband

Day 30

Dear future husband,

Today I thank God for giving our marriage new life. I proclaim that our marriage is alive and vibrant. I thank you in advance for the flowers, walks in the park, holding hands, kisses on the forehead, and other small gestures you do to breathe life into our relationship.

Thoughts:

Today thank your husband in advance for any of the things that you would like him to do in your marriage. Speak life and love into your relationship.

Verses:

Isaiah 43:18-19; 2 Corinthians 5:17

31 Day Devotional for Journaling to Your Future Husband

Day 31

Dear future husband,

I thank God for this journey. Each day as I write, I become closer to you and to God. The sacrifices and commitment that we make now to put God first will directly align us for His blessings. We are traveling this road together, so if we stay the course, we cannot miss each other. He is watching over our entire journey.

Thoughts:

God designed this journey to strengthen and prepare you for your husband. He has lessons in everything you encounter along the way. Writing to your husband daily should edify your spirit and keep you strong while traveling. This entire journey was designed to bring you closer to God and to your future husband.

Verse:

Deuteronomy 2:7

About the Author

Franda A. Clay is a native of Atlanta, Georgia. She resides there with her beautiful young adult daughters. Throughout her life, she endured the loss of her mother at age nine and the unexpected loss her husband at the age of 31, resulting in serious bouts of depression and anxiety. Both of these experiences pressed her to begin writing about her feelings as a way to cope with the losses. She says that, "It [writing] is my outlet. When I put pen to paper, I can see my path more clearly. It's like a roadmap to the future".

Her foundational Bible scripture is, none other than, Habakkuk 2:2-3, *"Then the Lord answered me and said, "Write the vision and engrave it plainly on [clay] tablets, so that the one who reads it will run. For the vision is yet for the appointed [future] time. It hurries toward the goal [of fulfillment]; it will not fail. Even though it delays, wait [patiently] for it, because it will certainly not delay."*

She is also passionate about helping and inspiring others through her personal experiences. As she states, "I believe God allows me to go through certain experiences in life so that I can create a story or give it a voice". When she is not writing, she uses her Master's degree to teach accounting and management courses at a local community college in Atlanta. In a few short months, she will become Dr. Franda A. Clay. Her hobbies include CrossFit and a number of other outdoor activities.

.

Made in the USA
Columbia, SC
06 August 2017